Car Sea :s

Great for when you're on the move with Baby, all these little covers are easy to crochet. Each can be made in two sizes based on your choice of yarn and hook size.

LEISURE ARTS, INC. • Maumelle, Arkansas

ALTERNATING BLOCKS

We have included a separate Finished Size, Shopping List and Gauge Information so you can make a larger blanket for older babies. Follow the same instructions, page 5, for both sizes.

■■□□▷ **EASY**

Finished Size: 16"w x 20½"h (40.5 cm x 52 cm)

SHOPPING LIST

Yarn (Light Weight)
[5 ounces, 395 yards (140 grams, 361 meters) per skein]:
☐ One skein
Crochet Hook
☐ Size G (4 mm) **or** size needed for gauge

Finished Size: 22½"w x 36"h (57 cm x 91.5 cm)

SHOPPING LIST

Yarn (Medium Weight)
[7 ounces, 390 yards (198 grams, 357 meters) per skein]:
☐ 2 skeins
Crochet Hook
☐ Size J (6 mm) **or** size needed for gauge

GAUGE INFORMATION

Using Light Weight Yarn
In pattern, 12 sts and 8 rows = 3" (7.5 cm)
Gauge Swatch: 3" (7.5 cm) square

Using Medium Weight Yarn
In pattern, 12 sts = 4¼" (10.75 cm) and 8 rows = 5¼" (13.25 cm)
Gauge Swatch: 4¼"w x 5¼"h (10.75 cm x 13.25 cm)

GAUGE SWATCH INSTRUCTIONS
Ch 14.
Row 1 (Right side)**:** Working in back ridges of beginning ch *(Fig. 3, page 46)*, dc in fourth ch from hook **(3 skipped chs count as first dc)** and in each ch across: 12 dc.
Row 2: Ch 1, turn; sc in each dc across.
Row 3: Ch 3 **(counts as first dc)**, turn; dc in next sc and in each sc across.
Rows 4-8: Repeat Rows 2 and 3 twice, then repeat Row 2 once **more**: 12 sc. Finish off.

INSTRUCTIONS
Blanket

Ch 65.

Row 1 (Right side): Working in back ridges of beginning ch *(Fig. 3, page 46)*, dc in fourth ch from hook **(3 skipped chs count as first dc)** and in each ch across: 63 dc.

Row 2: Ch 1, turn; sc in each dc across.

Row 3: Ch 3 **(counts as first dc, now and throughout)**, turn; dc in next sc and in each sc across.

Row 4: Ch 1, turn; sc in each dc across.

Row 5: Ch 3, turn; dc in next 6 sc, ch 1, skip next sc, (dc in next 3 sc, ch 1, skip next sc) 4 times, dc in next 15 sc, ch 1, skip next sc, (dc in next 3 sc, ch 1, skip next sc) 4 times, dc in last 7 sc: 53 dc and 10 ch-1 sps.

Row 6: Ch 1, turn; sc in first 7 dc and in next ch-1 sp, (ch 3, skip next 3 dc, sc in next ch-1 sp) 4 times, sc in next 15 dc and in next ch-1 sp, (ch 3, skip next 3 dc, sc in next ch-1 sp) 4 times, sc in last 7 dc: 39 sc and 24 chs.

Row 7: Ch 3, turn; dc in next 6 sc, ch 1, skip next sc, (dc in next 3 chs, ch 1, skip next sc) 4 times, dc in next 15 sc, ch 1, skip next sc, (dc in next 3 chs, ch 1, skip next sc) 4 times, dc in last 7 sc: 53 dc and 10 ch-1 sps.

Rows 8-15: Repeat Rows 6 and 7, 4 times: 53 dc and 10 ch-1 sps.

Row 16: Ch 1, turn; sc in first 7 dc and in next ch-1 sp, (sc in next 3 dc and in next ch-1 sp) 4 times, ch 3, skip next 3 dc, (sc in next dc, ch 3, skip next 3 dc) 3 times, sc in next ch-1 sp, (sc in next 3 dc and in next ch-1 sp) 4 times, sc in last 7 dc: 51 sc and 12 chs.

Row 17: Ch 3, turn; dc in next 6 sc, ch 1, skip next sc, dc in next 15 sc, ch 1, skip next sc, (dc in next 3 chs, ch 1, skip next sc) 4 times, dc in next 15 sc, ch 1, skip next sc, dc in last 7 sc: 56 dc and 7 ch-1 sps.

Row 18: Ch 1, turn; sc in first 7 dc and in next ch-1 sp, sc in next 15 dc and in next ch-1 sp, (ch 3, skip next 3 dc, sc in next ch-1 sp) 4 times, sc in next 15 dc and in next ch-1 sp, sc in last 7 dc: 51 sc and 12 chs.

Rows 19-27: Repeat Rows 17 and 18, 4 times; then repeat Row 17 once **more**: 56 dc and 7 ch-1 sps.

Row 28: Ch 1, turn; sc in first 7 dc and in next ch-1 sp, ch 3, skip next 3 dc, (sc in next dc, ch 3, skip next 3 dc) 3 times, sc in next ch-1 sp, (sc in next 3 dc and in next ch-1 sp) 4 times, ch 3, skip next 3 dc, (sc in next dc, ch 3, skip next 3 dc) 3 times, sc in next ch-1 sp and in last 7 dc: 39 sc and 24 chs.

Row 29: Ch 3, turn; dc in next 6 sc, ch 1, skip next sc, (dc in next 3 chs, ch 1, skip next sc) 4 times, dc in next 15 sc, ch 1, skip next sc, (dc in next 3 chs, ch 1, skip next sc) 4 times, dc in last 7 sc: 53 dc and 10 ch-1 sps.

Rows 30-51: Repeat Rows 6-27: 56 dc and 7 ch-1 sps.

Row 52: Ch 1, turn; sc in first 7 dc and in next ch-1 sp, sc in next 15 dc and in next ch-1 sp, (sc in next 3 dc and in next ch-1 sp) 4 times, sc in next 15 dc and in next ch-1 sp, sc in last 7 dc: 63 sc.

Row 53: Ch 3, turn; dc in next sc and in each sc across.

Row 54: Ch 1, turn; sc in each dc across.

Row 55: Ch 3, turn; dc in next sc and in each sc across; finish off.

LEAF STITCH

We have included a separate Finished Size, Shopping List and Gauge Information so you can make a larger blanket for older babies. Follow the same instructions, page 11, for both sizes.

◖■■☐☐◗ **EASY**

Finished Size: 16¾"w x 21¼"h (42.5 cm x 54 cm)

SHOPPING LIST

Yarn (Light Weight)
[5 ounces, 395 yards (140 grams, 361 meters) per skein]:
☐ One skein
Crochet Hook
☐ Size G (4 mm) **or** size needed for gauge

Finished Size: 25"w x 29"h (63.5 cm x 73.5 cm)

SHOPPING LIST

Yarn (Medium Weight)
[7 ounces, 390 yards (198 grams, 357 meters) per skein]:
☐ 2 skeins
Crochet Hook
☐ Size J (6 mm) **or** size needed for gauge

GAUGE INFORMATION

Using Light Weight Yarn
In pattern, 14 sts and 8½ rows = 4" (10 cm)
Gauge Swatch: 5"w x 3¾"h (12.75 cm x 9.5 cm)

Using Medium Weight Yarn
In pattern, 14 sts = 6" (15.25 cm) and 8½ rows = 5½" (14 cm)
Gauge Swatch: 6"w x 5¼"h (15.25 cm x 13.25 cm)

GAUGE SWATCH INSTRUCTIONS
Ch 19.
Work same as Blanket for 8 rows: 17 sts.
Finish off.

── STITCH GUIDE ──

LEAF ST

YO, † insert hook from **front** to **back** around post of **next** dc *(Fig. 6, page 47)*, YO and pull up a loop even with loops on hook, YO, insert hook from **front** to **back** around post of **same** dc, YO and pull up a loop even with loops on hook, YO and draw through 4 loops on hook †, YO, skip next dc, repeat from † to † once, YO and draw through all 3 loops on hook.

INSTRUCTIONS
Blanket

Ch 59.

Row 1 (Right side)**:** Dc in fourth ch from hook **(3 skipped chs count as first dc)** and in each ch across: 57 dc.

Row 2: Ch 3 **(counts as first dc, now and throughout)**, turn; dc in next dc and in each dc across.

Row 3: Ch 3, turn; dc in next 3 dc, ★ work Leaf St, working **behind** Leaf St, skip next dc from last dc made and dc in next 3 dc; repeat from ★ across to last 5 dc, work Leaf St, working **behind** Leaf St, skip next dc from last dc made and dc in last 4 dc: 44 dc and 13 Leaf Sts.

Rows 4-6: Ch 3, turn; dc in next st and in each st across: 57 dc.

Rows 7-44: Repeat Rows 3-6, 9 times; then repeat Rows 3 and 4 once **more**.

Edging: Ch 1, turn; sc evenly around entire Blanket working 3 sc in each corner; join with slip st to first sc, finish off.

MOUNTAINS & VALLEYS

We have included a separate Finished Size, Shopping List and Gauge Information so you can make a larger blanket for older babies. Follow the same instructions, page 16, for both sizes.

 **EASY**

Finished Size: 16"w x 21¼"h (40.5 cm x 54 cm)

SHOPPING LIST

Yarn (Light Weight) 🧶 3 LIGHT
[5 ounces, 395 yards (140 grams, 361 meters) per skein]:
- ☐ Pink - One skein
- ☐ Blue - One skein
- ☐ White - One skein
- ☐ Green - One skein
- ☐ Yellow - One skein

Crochet Hook
- ☐ Size G (4 mm) **or** size needed for gauge

Finished Size: 22¾"w x 30"h (58 cm x 76 cm)

SHOPPING LIST

Yarn (Medium Weight) 🧶 4 MEDIUM
[7 ounces, 390 yards (198 grams, 357 meters) per skein]:
- ☐ Pink - One skein
- ☐ Blue - One skein
- ☐ White - One skein
- ☐ Green - One skein
- ☐ Yellow - One skein

Crochet Hook
- ☐ Size J (6 mm) **or** size needed for gauge

GAUGE INFORMATION

Using Light Weight Yarn
In pattern, 2 repeats = 3½" (9 cm) and 12 rows = 4¼" (10.75 cm)
Gauge Swatch: 3¾"w x 2⅛"h (9.5 cm x 5.5 cm)

Using Medium Weight Yarn
In pattern, 2 repeats = 5" (12.75 cm) and 12 rows = 6" (15.25 cm)
Gauge Swatch: 5¼"w x 3"h (13.25 cm x 7.5 cm)

GAUGE SWATCH INSTRUCTIONS
With Pink, ch 14.
Work same as Blanket, page 16, for 6 rows (do **not** change colors at end of Row 6): 13 sc.
Finish off.

STITCH GUIDE

TREBLE CROCHET *(abbreviated tr)*

YO twice, insert hook in sc indicated, YO and pull up a loop (4 loops on hook), (YO and draw through 2 loops on hook) 3 times.

SINGLE CROCHET 2 TOGETHER
(abbreviated sc2tog)

Pull up a loop in each of next 2 sts, YO and draw through all 3 loops on hook (**counts as one sc**).

SINGLE CROCHET 3 TOGETHER
(abbreviated sc3tog)

Pull up a loop in each of next 3 sts, YO and draw through all 4 loops on hook (**counts as one sc**).

TREBLE CROCHET 2 TOGETHER
(abbreviated tr2tog)
(uses next 2 sc)

★ YO twice, insert hook in **next** sc, YO and pull up a loop, (YO and draw through 2 loops on hook) twice; repeat from ★ once **more**, YO and draw through all 3 loops on hook.

TREBLE CROCHET 3 TOGETHER
(abbreviated tr3tog)
(uses next 3 sc)

★ YO twice, insert hook in **next** sc, YO and pull up a loop, (YO and draw through 2 loops on hook) twice; repeat from ★ 2 times **more**, YO and draw through all 4 loops on hook.

INSTRUCTIONS
Blanket

The entire Blanket is worked in the following stripe sequence, changing colors every 2 rows (*Fig. 5, page 47*): ★ Pink, Blue, White, Green, Yellow; repeat from ★ for sequence.

With Pink, ch 56.

Row 1 (Right side)**:** Working in back ridges of beginning ch (*Fig. 3, page 46)*, sc in second ch from hook and in each ch across: 55 sc.

Row 2: Ch 1, turn; sc in first sc, ★ hdc in next sc, dc in next sc, 3 tr in next sc, dc in next sc, hdc in next sc, sc in next sc; repeat from ★ across changing to next color in last sc made: 73 sts.

Row 3: Ch 1, turn; skip first sc, sc in next 3 sts, 3 sc in next st, sc in next 2 sts, ★ sc3tog, sc in next 2 sts, 3 sc in next st, sc in next 2 sts; repeat from ★ across to last 2 sts, sc2 tog.

Row 4: Ch 1, turn; skip first sc, sc in next 3 sc, 3 sc in next sc, sc in next 2 sc, ★ sc3tog, sc in next 2 sc, 3 sc in next sc, sc in next 2 sc; repeat from ★ across to last 2 sc, sc2 tog changing to next color.

Row 5: Ch 3 (does **not** count as a st), turn; skip first sc, tr in next sc, dc in next sc, hdc in next sc, sc in next sc, hdc in next sc, dc in next sc, ★ tr3tog, dc in next sc, hdc in next sc, sc in next sc, hdc in next sc, dc in next sc; repeat from ★ across to last 2 sc, tr2tog: 55 sts.

Row 6: Ch 1, turn; sc in each st across to last tr, sc in last tr changing to next color.

Row 7: Ch 1, turn; sc in each sc across.

Rows 8-59: Repeat Rows 2-7, 8 times; then repeat Rows 2-5 once **more**: 55 sts.

Row 60: Ch 1, turn; sc in each st across ending in last tr; finish off.

RECTANGULAR FILET

Shown on page 19.

We have included a separate Finished Size, Shopping List and Gauge Information so you can make a larger blanket for older babies. Follow the same instructions, page 18, for both sizes.

 **EASY**

Finished Size: 16"w x 19½"h (40.5 cm x 49.5 cm)

SHOPPING LIST

Yarn (Light Weight) **(3)**
[5 ounces, 395 yards (140 grams, 361 meters) per skein]:
☐ One skein
Crochet Hook
☐ Size G (4 mm) **or** size needed for gauge

Finished Size: 21"w x 24½"h (53.5 cm x 62 cm)

SHOPPING LIST

Yarn (Medium Weight) **(4)**
[7 ounces, 390 yards (198 grams, 357 meters) per skein]:
☐ 2 skeins
Crochet Hook
☐ Size J (6 mm) **or** size needed for gauge

GAUGE INFORMATION

Using Light Weight Yarn
Gauge Swatch: 2¾"w x 5¾"h (7 cm x 14.5 cm)

Using Medium Weight Yarn
Gauge Swatch: 3½"w x 7"h (9 cm x 17.75 cm)

GAUGE SWATCH INSTRUCTIONS
Work same as Blanket through Rnd 4: 26 dc and 26 sps.

INSTRUCTIONS
Blanket
Ch 14.

Rnd 1 (Right side): Sc in second ch from hook and in next 11 chs, 3 sc in last ch; working in free loops of beginning ch *(Fig. 4, page 47)*, sc in next 11 chs, 2 sc in next ch; join with slip st to first sc: 28 sc.

Rnd 2: Ch 1, sc in same st as joining and in next 11 sc, (sc, ch 3, sc) in next sc, sc in next sc, (sc, ch 3, sc) in next sc, sc in next 11 sc, (sc, ch 3, sc) in next sc, sc in next sc and in same st as first sc, ch 3; join with slip st to first sc: 32 sc and 4 ch-3 sps.

Rnd 3: Ch 1, sc in same st as joining and in next 12 sc, (sc, ch 3, sc) in next ch-3 sp, sc in next 3 sc, (sc, ch 3, sc) in next ch-3 sp, sc in next 13 sc, (sc, ch 3, sc) in next ch-3 sp, sc in next 3 sc, (sc, ch 3, sc) in next ch-3 sp; join with slip st to first sc: 40 sc and 4 ch-3 sps.

Rnd 4 (Wrong side)**:** Ch 4 (**counts as first dc plus ch 1, now and throughout**), **turn**; skip next sc, (dc, ch 3, dc) in next ch-3 sp, ch 1, skip next sc, (dc in next sc, ch 1, skip next sc) twice, (dc, ch 3, dc) in next ch-3 sp, ch 1, skip next sc, (dc in next sc, ch 1, skip next sc) 7 times, (dc, ch 3, dc) in next ch-3 sp, ch 1, skip next sc, (dc in next sc, ch 1, skip next sc) twice, (dc, ch 3, dc) in next ch-3 sp, ch 1, skip next sc, (dc in next sc, ch 1, skip next sc) 6 times; join with slip st to first dc: 26 dc and 26 sps.

Rnd 5 (Right side)**:** Ch 1, **turn**; sc in same st as joining, (sc in next ch-1 sp and in next dc) across to next ch-3 sp, (sc, ch 3, sc) in ch-3 sp (corner made), sc in next dc, ★ (sc in next ch-1 sp and in next dc) across to next ch-3 sp, (sc, ch 3, sc) in ch-3 sp (corner made), sc in next dc; repeat from ★ 2 times **more**, sc in last ch-1 sp; join with slip st to first sc: 56 sc and 4 corner ch-3 sps.

Rnds 6 and 7: Ch 1, do **not** turn; sc in same st as joining, ★ sc in next sc and in each sc across to next corner ch-3 sp, (sc, ch 3, sc) in corner sp; repeat from ★ 3 times **more**, sc in next sc and in each sc across; join with slip st to first sc: 72 sc and 4 corner ch-3 sps.

Rnd 8 (Wrong side)**:** Ch 4, **turn**; ★ skip next sc, (dc in next sc, ch 1, skip next sc) across to next corner ch-3 sp, (dc, ch 3, dc) in corner sp, ch 1; repeat from ★ 3 times **more**, skip next sc, (dc in next sc, ch 1, skip next sc) across; join with slip st to first dc: 42 dc and 42 sps.

Rnd 9 (Right side)**:** Ch 1, **turn**; sc in same st as joining, ★ (sc in next ch-1 sp and in next dc) across to next ch-3 sp, (sc, ch 3, sc) in ch-3 sp (corner made), sc in next dc; repeat from ★ 3 times **more**, sc in next ch-1 sp, (sc in next dc and in next ch-1 sp) across; join with slip st to first sc: 88 sc and 4 corner ch-3 sps.

Rnds 10-27: Repeat Rnds 6-9, 4 times; then repeat Rnds 6 and 7 once **more**: 232 sc and 4 corner ch-3 sps.

Rnd 28 (Right side)**:** Ch 1, do **not** turn; working from **left** to **right**, ★ insert hook in sc to right of hook *(Fig. 1a)*, YO and draw through, under and to the left of loop on hook (2 loops on hook) *(Fig. 1b)*, YO and draw through both loops on hook *(Fig. 1c)* (reverse sc made, *Fig. 1d)*; repeat from ★ around, working 3 reverse sc in each corner ch-3 sp; join with slip st to first st, finish off.

Fig. 1a

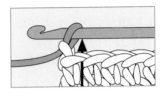

Fig. 1b

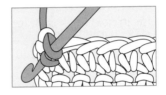

Fig. 1c

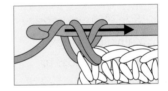

Fig. 1d

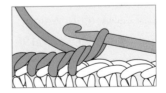

RIPPLE

We have included a separate Finished Size, Shopping List and Gauge Information so you can make a larger blanket for older babies. Follow the same instructions, page 27, for both sizes.

 **EASY**

Finished Size: 16½"w x 21"h (42 cm x 53.5 cm)

SHOPPING LIST

Yarn (Light Weight) 🧶 **3** LIGHT

[5 ounces, 395 yards (140 grams, 361 meters) per skein]:
- ☐ Blue - One skein
- ☐ Pink - One skein
- ☐ White - One skein

Crochet Hook
- ☐ Size G (4 mm) **or** size needed for gauge

Finished Size: 22½"w x 27¾"h (57 cm x 70.5 cm)

SHOPPING LIST

Yarn (Medium Weight) 🧶 **4** MEDIUM

[7 ounces, 390 yards (198 grams, 357 meters) per skein]:
- ☐ Blue - One skein
- ☐ Pink - One skein
- ☐ White - One skein

Crochet Hook
- ☐ Size J (6 mm) **or** size needed for gauge

GAUGE INFORMATION

Using Light Weight Yarn

In pattern, one repeat (point-to-point) = 5½" (14 cm) and
8 rows = 4½" (11.5 cm)

Gauge Swatch: 16½"w x 4½"h (42 cm x 11.5 cm)

Using Medium Weight Yarn

In pattern, one repeat (point-to-point) = 7½" (19 cm) and
8 rows = 6" (15.25 cm)

Gauge Swatch: 22½"w x 6"h (57 cm x 15.25 cm)

GAUGE SWATCH INSTRUCTIONS

Work same as Blanket, page 27, for 8 rows: 27 ch-3 sps.

MEASURING YOUR GAUGE & YOUR BLANKET

Lay your piece on a flat hard surface.

Measure one point-to-point repeat by placing the ruler from the center of one "peak" increase to the center of the next "peak" increase.

Measure the height of your gauge swatch by placing the ruler from the bottom of the center stitch of a "peak" increase to the highest point of the swatch.

Measure the width of your gauge swatch or Blanket from straight edge to straight edge. The length of the Blanket is measured from the bottom of the lowest "valley" to the top of the highest "peak".

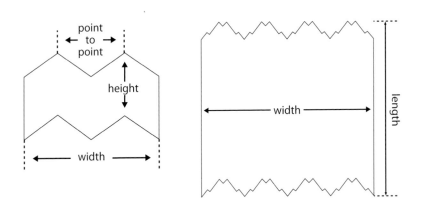

STITCH GUIDE

BEGINNING SINGLE CROCHET 3 TOGETHER
(abbreviated beginning sc3tog)
(uses first 3 sts)

Pull up a loop in first dc, in next ch-1 sp, and in next dc, YO and draw through all 4 loops on hook (**counts as one sc**).

SINGLE CROCHET 3 TOGETHER
(abbreviated sc3tog)
(uses next 3 sts)

Pull up a loop in next dc, in next ch-1 sp, and in next dc, YO and draw through all 4 loops on hook (**counts as one sc**).

SINGLE CROCHET 4 TOGETHER
(abbreviated sc4tog) (uses next dc, next 2 ch-1 sps, & next dc)

Pull up a loop in next dc, in each of next 2 ch-1 sps, and in next dc, YO and draw through all 5 loops on hook (**counts as one sc**).

DOUBLE CROCHET 2 TOGETHER
(abbreviated dc2tog)
(uses next 2 sts)

★ YO, insert hook in **next** st, YO and pull up a loop, YO and draw through 2 loops on hook; repeat from ★ once **more**, YO and draw through all 3 loops on hook (**counts as one dc**).

DOUBLE CROCHET 3 TOGETHER
(abbreviated dc3tog)
(uses next 3 sts)

★ YO, insert hook in **next** st, YO and pull up a loop, YO and draw through 2 loops on hook; repeat from ★ 2 times **more**, YO and draw through all 4 loops on hook (**counts as one dc**).

INSTRUCTIONS
Blanket

With White, ch 80.

Row 1 (Right side): Dc in third ch from hook, ch 1, skip next 2 chs, (3 dc in next ch, ch 1, skip next 2 chs) 3 times, (3 dc, ch 3, 3 dc) in next ch, ch 1, (skip next 2 chs, 3 dc in next ch, ch 1) 3 times, skip next 2 chs, ★ dc3tog, ch 1, skip next 2 chs, (3 dc in next ch, ch 1, skip next 2 chs) 3 times, (3 dc, ch 3, 3 dc) in next ch, ch 1, (skip next 2 chs, 3 dc in next ch, ch 1) 3 times, skip next 2 chs; repeat from ★ once **more**, dc2tog; finish off: 76 dc and 27 sps.

Note: Loop a short piece of yarn around any stitch to mark Row 1 as **right** side.

Row 2: With **right** side facing, join Blue with slip st in first dc; ch 1, work beginning sc3tog, ch 3, skip next dc, (sc3tog, ch 3, skip next dc) 3 times, pull up a loop in next dc and in next ch-3 sp, YO and draw through all 3 loops on hook, ch 3, pull up a loop in same ch-3 sp and in next dc, YO and draw through all 3 loops on hook, ch 3, skip next dc, ★ (sc3tog, ch 3, skip next dc) 3 times, sc4tog, ch 3, skip next dc, (sc3tog, ch 3, skip next dc) 3 times, pull up a loop in next dc and in next ch-3 sp, YO and draw through all 3 loops on hook, ch 3, pull up a loop in same ch-3 sp and in next dc, YO and draw through all 3 loops on hook, ch 3, skip next dc; repeat from ★ once **more**, sc3tog, (ch 3, skip next dc, sc3tog) 3 times: 27 ch-3 sps.

Row 3: Ch 2, turn; dc in next ch-3 sp, ch 1, (3 dc in next ch-3 sp, ch 1) 3 times, (3 dc, ch 3, 3 dc) in next ch-3 sp, ch 1, (3 dc in next ch-3 sp, ch 1) 3 times, ★ dc in next ch-3 sp, [YO, insert hook in **same** sp, YO and pull up a loop, YO and draw through 2 loops on hook, YO, insert hook in **next** ch-3 sp, YO and pull up a loop, YO and draw through 2 loops on hook, YO and draw through all 3 loops on hook **(counts as one dc)]**, dc in same ch-3 sp, ch 1, (3 dc in next ch-3 sp, ch 1) 3 times, (3 dc, ch 3, 3 dc) in next ch-3 sp, ch 1, (3 dc in next ch-3 sp, ch 1) 3 times; repeat from ★ once **more**, [YO, insert hook in last ch-3 sp, YO and pull up a loop, YO and draw through 2 loops on hook, YO, insert hook in last sc, YO and pull up a loop, YO and draw through 2 loops on hook, YO and draw through all 3 loops on hook **(counts as one dc)]**: 80 dc and 27 sps.

Row 4: Ch 1, turn; work beginning sc3tog, ch 3, skip next dc, (sc3tog, ch 3, skip next dc) 3 times, pull up a loop in next dc and in next ch-3 sp, YO and draw through all 3 loops on hook, ch 3, pull up a loop in same ch-3 sp and in next dc, YO and draw through all 3 loops on hook, ch 3, skip next dc, ★ (sc3tog, ch 3, skip next dc) 3 times, sc4tog, ch 3, skip next dc, (sc3tog, ch 3, skip next dc) 3 times, pull up a loop in next dc and in next ch-3 sp, YO and draw through all 3 loops on hook, ch 3, pull up a loop in same ch-3 sp and in next dc, YO and draw through all 3 loops on hook, ch 3, skip next dc; repeat from ★ once **more**, sc3tog, (ch 3, skip next dc, sc3tog) 3 times; finish off: 27 ch-3 sps.

Row 5: With **right** side facing, join White with slip st in first sc; ch 2, dc in next ch-3 sp, ch 1, (3 dc in next ch-3 sp, ch 1) 3 times, (3 dc, ch 3, 3 dc) in next ch-3 sp, ch 1, (3 dc in next ch-3 sp, ch 1) 3 times, ★ dc in next ch-3 sp, [YO, insert hook in **same** sp, YO and pull up a loop, YO and draw through 2 loops on hook, YO, insert hook in **next** ch-3 sp, YO and pull up a loop, YO and draw through 2 loops on hook, YO and draw through all 3 loops on hook **(counts as one dc)]**, dc in same ch-3 sp, ch 1, (3 dc in next ch-3 sp, ch 1) 3 times, (3 dc, ch 3, 3 dc) in next ch-3 sp, ch 1, (3 dc in next ch-3 sp, ch 1) 3 times; repeat from ★ once **more**, [YO, insert hook in last ch-3 sp, YO and pull up a loop, YO and draw through 2 loops on hook, YO, insert hook in last sc, YO and pull up a loop, YO and draw through 2 loops on hook, YO and draw through all 3 loops on hook **(counts as one dc)]**; finish off: 80 dc and 27 sps.

Rows 6-8: With Pink, repeat Rows 2-4: 27 ch-3 sps.

Row 9: Repeat Row 5: 80 dc and 27 sps.

Rows 10-37: Repeat Rows 2-9, 3 times; then repeat Rows 2-5 once **more**.

VERTICAL STRIPES

We have included a separate Finished Size, Shopping List and Gauge Information so you can make a larger blanket for older babies. Follow the same instructions, page 33, for both sizes.

■■□□ **EASY**

Finished Size: 17½"w x 20"h (44.5 cm x 51 cm)

SHOPPING LIST

Yarn (Light Weight) **3**

[5 ounces, 395 yards (140 grams, 361 meters) per skein]:
- ☐ Yellow - One skein
- ☐ White - One skein
- ☐ Green - One skein

Crochet Hook

- ☐ Size G (4 mm) **or** size needed for gauge

Finished Size: 25"w x 24"h (63.5 cm x 61 cm)

SHOPPING LIST

Yarn (Medium Weight) **4**

[7 ounces, 390 yards (198 grams, 357 meters) per skein]:
- ☐ Yellow - One skein
- ☐ White - One skein
- ☐ Green - One skein

Crochet Hook

- ☐ Size J (6 mm) **or** size needed for gauge

GAUGE INFORMATION

Using Light Weight Yarn

In pattern, (sc, ch 1, dc) 6 times = 3¾" (9.5 cm) and 12 rows = 4" (10 cm)

Gauge Swatch: 4¼"w x 4"h (10.75 cm x 10 cm)

Using Medium Weight Yarn

In pattern, (sc, ch 1, dc) 6 times = 4½" (11.5 cm) and 12 rows = 5¾" (14.5 cm)

Gauge Swatch: 5¼"w x 5¾"h (13.25 cm x 14.5 cm)

GAUGE SWATCH INSTRUCTIONS

With Yellow, ch 14 **loosely**.

Work same as Blanket for 12 rows: 14 sts.

Finish off.

INSTRUCTIONS

Blanket is worked from side-to-side, crocheting across length of piece.

Blanket

With Yellow, ch 64 **loosely**; place a marker in second ch from hook for trim placement.

Row 1 (Right side)**:** (Sc, ch 1, dc) in second ch from hook, ★ skip next ch, (sc, ch 1, dc) in next ch; repeat from ★ across: 64 sts and 32 ch-1 sps.

Note: Loop a short piece of yarn around any stitch to mark Row 1 as **right** side.

Rows 2 and 3: Ch 1, turn; ★ skip next ch-1 sp, (sc, ch 1, dc) in Back Loop Only of next sc *(Fig. 2, page 46)*; repeat from ★ across.

Finish off.

Row 4: With **wrong** side facing, skip first dc and next ch-1 sp and join White with sc in Back Loop Only of next sc *(see Joining With Sc, page 46)*; ch 1, dc in same st, ★ skip next ch-1 sp, (sc, ch 1, dc) in Back Loop Only of next sc; repeat from ★ across.

Row 5: Ch 1, turn; ★ skip next ch-1 sp, (sc, ch 1, dc) in Back Loop Only of next sc; repeat from ★ across; finish off.

Row 6: With **wrong** side facing, skip first dc and next ch-1 sp and join Green with sc in Back Loop Only of next sc; ch 1, dc in same st, ★ skip next ch-1 sp, (sc, ch 1, dc) in Back Loop Only of next sc; repeat from ★ across.

Rows 7-9: Ch 1, turn; ★ skip next ch-1 sp, (sc, ch 1, dc) in Back Loop Only of next sc; repeat from ★ across; at end of last row, finish off.

Row 10: With **wrong** side facing, skip first dc and next ch-1 sp and join White with sc in Back Loop Only of next sc; ch 1, dc in same st, ★ skip next ch-1 sp, (sc, ch 1, dc) in Back Loop Only of next sc; repeat from ★ across.

Row 11: Ch 1, turn; ★ skip next ch-1 sp, (sc, ch 1, dc) in Back Loop Only of next sc; repeat from ★ across; finish off.

Row 12: With **wrong** side facing, skip first dc and next ch-1 sp and join Yellow with sc in Back Loop Only of next sc; ch 1, dc in same st, ★ skip next ch-1 sp, (sc, ch 1, dc) in Back Loop Only of next sc; repeat from ★ across.

Rows 13-15: Ch 1, turn; ★ skip next ch-1 sp, (sc, ch 1, dc) in Back Loop Only of next sc; repeat from ★ across; at end of last row, finish off.

Rows 16-51: Repeat Rows 4-15, 3 times.

Trim: With **right** side facing, join Yellow with sc in free loop of first ch *(Fig. 4, page 47)*; ch 1, dc in same st, working in back loops of skipped chs on Row 1, ★ (sc, ch 1, dc) in next ch, skip free loop of next ch; repeat from ★ across to marked ch, (sc, ch 1, dc) in marked ch; finish off.

CROSSED DOUBLES

Shown on page 37.

We have included a separate Finished Size, Shopping List and Gauge Information so you can make a larger blanket for older babies. Follow the same instructions, page 38, for both sizes.

 **EASY**

Finished Size: 16"w x 21"h (40.5 cm x 53.5 cm)

SHOPPING LIST

Yarn (Light Weight) 🧶3 LIGHT
[5 ounces, 395 yards (140 grams, 361 meters) per skein]:
☐ One skein

Crochet Hook
☐ Size G (4 mm) **or** size needed for gauge

Finished Size: 22"w x 29¾"h (56.5 cm x 75.5 cm)

SHOPPING LIST

Yarn (Medium Weight) 🧶4 MEDIUM
[7 ounces, 390 yards (198 grams, 357 meters) per skein]:
☐ 2 skeins

Crochet Hook
☐ Size J (6 mm) **or** size needed for gauge

GAUGE INFORMATION

Using Light Weight Yarn

16 dc = 4¹/₈" (10.5 cm) and 10 rows = 4¾" (12 cm)

Gauge Swatch: 4¹/₈"w x 4¾"h (10.5 cm x 12 cm)

Using Medium Weight Yarn

16 dc = 5¾" (14.5 cm) and 10 rows = 6¾" (17.25 cm)

Gauge Swatch: 5¾"w x 6¾"h (14.5 cm x 17.25 cm)

GAUGE SWATCH INSTRUCTIONS

Ch 18.

Row 1: Working in back ridges of beginning ch *(Fig. 3, page 46)*, dc in fourth ch from hook (**3 skipped chs count as first dc**) and in each ch across: 16 dc.

Rows 2-10: Ch 3 (**counts as first dc**), turn; dc in next dc and in each dc across.

Finish off.

STITCH GUIDE

CROSS ST (uses next 2 dc)
Skip next dc, dc in next dc,
working **behind** last dc made, dc in
skipped dc.

INSTRUCTIONS
Blanket
Ch 64.

Row 1 (Wrong side)**:** Working in
back ridges of beginning ch *(Fig. 3,
page 46)*, dc in fourth ch from hook
(3 skipped chs count as first dc)
and in each ch across: 62 dc.

Rows 2 and 3: Ch 3 **(counts as first
dc, now and throughout)**, turn; dc
in next dc and in each dc across.

Rows 4-41: Ch 3, turn; dc in next
4 dc, work 26 Cross Sts, dc in last
5 dc.

Rows 42-44: Ch 3, turn; dc in next
dc and in each dc across.

Finish off.

ZIG ZAG FILET

Shown on page 41.

We have included a separate Finished Size, Shopping List and Gauge Information so you can make a larger blanket for older babies. Follow the same instructions, page 42, for both sizes.

 **EASY**

Finished Size: 16½"w x 22½"h (42 cm x 57 cm)

SHOPPING LIST

Yarn (Light Weight)
[5 ounces, 395 yards (140 grams, 361 meters) per skein]:
☐ One skein

Crochet Hook
☐ Size G (4 mm) **or** size needed for gauge

Finished Size: 22¼"w x 28¾"h (56.5 cm x 73 cm)

SHOPPING LIST

Yarn (Medium Weight)
[7 ounces, 390 yards (198 grams, 357 meters) per skein]:
☐ 2 skeins

Crochet Hook
☐ Size J (6 mm) **or** size needed for gauge

GAUGE INFORMATION

Using Light Weight Yarn
In pattern, 20 sts and 9 rows = 4½" (11.5 cm)
Gauge Swatch: 4½" (11.5 cm) square

Using Medium Weight Yarn
In pattern, 20 sts = 6" (15.25 cm) and 9 rows = 5¾" (14.5 cm)
Gauge Swatch: 6"w x 5¾"h (15.25 cm x 14.5 cm)

GAUGE SWATCH INSTRUCTIONS
Ch 22.
Work same as Blanket, page 42, for 9 rows: 16 dc and 4 chs (20 sts total).
Finish off.

INSTRUCTIONS
Blanket

Ch 76.

Row 1: Working in back ridges of beginning ch *(Fig. 3, page 46)*, dc in fourth ch from hook (**3 skipped chs count as first dc**) and in each ch across: 74 dc.

Row 2 (Right side)**:** Ch 3 (**counts as first dc, now and throughout**), turn; dc in next dc and in each dc across.

Row 3: Ch 3, turn; dc in next 3 dc, ch 2, ★ skip next 2 dc, dc in next 4 dc, ch 2; repeat from ★ across to last 10 dc, skip next 2 dc, dc in last 8 dc: 52 dc and 22 chs (74 sts total).

Row 4: Ch 3, turn; dc in next 6 dc, ch 2, ★ skip next dc and next ch, dc in next ch and in next 3 dc, ch 2; repeat from ★ across to last 7 sts, skip next dc and next ch, dc in next ch and in last 4 dc.

Row 5: Ch 3, turn; dc in next 4 dc and in next ch, ch 2, ★ skip next ch and next dc, dc in next 3 dc and in next ch, ch 2; repeat from ★ across to last 8 sts, skip next ch and next dc, dc in last 6 dc.

Row 6: Ch 3, turn; dc in next 4 dc, ch 2, ★ skip next dc and next ch, dc in next ch and in next 3 dc, ch 2; repeat from ★ across to last 9 sts, skip next dc and next ch, dc in next ch and in last 6 dc.

Row 7: Ch 3, turn; dc in next 6 dc and in next ch, ch 2, ★ skip next ch and next dc, dc in next 3 dc and in next ch, ch 2; repeat from ★ across to last 6 sts, skip next ch and next dc, dc in last 4 dc.

Row 8: Ch 3, turn; dc in next 3 dc and in next ch, ch 2, ★ skip next ch and next dc, dc in next 3 dc and in next ch, ch 2; repeat from ★ across to last 9 sts, skip next ch and next dc, dc in last 7 dc.

Row 9: Ch 3, turn; dc in next 5 dc, ch 2, ★ skip next dc and next ch, dc in next ch and in next 3 dc, ch 2; repeat from ★ across to last 8 sts, skip next dc and next ch, dc in next ch and last 5 dc.

Row 10: Ch 3, turn; dc in next 5 dc and in next ch, ch 2, ★ skip next ch and next dc, dc in next 3 dc and in next ch, ch 2; repeat from ★ across to last 7 sts, skip next ch and next dc, dc in last 5 dc.

Row 11: Ch 3, turn; dc in next 3 dc, ch 2, ★ skip next dc and next ch, dc in next ch and in next 3 dc, ch 2; repeat from ★ across to last 10 sts, skip next dc and next ch, dc in next ch and in last 7 dc.

Rows 12-43: Repeat Rows 4-11, 4 times.

Row 44: Ch 3, turn; dc in next 7 dc, (dc in next 2 chs, dc in next 4 dc) across: 74 dc.

Row 45: Ch 3, turn; dc in next dc and in each dc across; finish off.

GENERAL INSTRUCTIONS

ABBREVIATIONS

ch(s)	chain(s)
cm	centimeters
dc	double crochet(s)
dc2tog	double crochet 2 together
dc3tog	double crochet 3 together
hdc	half double crochet(s)
mm	millimeters
Rnd(s)	Round(s)
sc	single crochet(s)
sc2tog	single crochet 2 together
sc3tog	single crochet 3 together
sc4tog	single crochet 4 together
sp(s)	space(s)
st(s)	stitch(es)
tr	treble crochet(s)
tr2tog	treble crochet 2 together
tr3tog	treble crochet 3 together
YO	yarn over

SYMBOLS & TERMS

★ — work instructions following ★ as many **more** times as indicated in addition to the first time.

( ) or **[ ]** — work enclosed instructions **as many** times as specified by the number immediately following **or** work all enclosed instructions in the stitch or space indicated **or** contains explanatory remarks.

colon (:) — the number(s) given after a colon at the end of a row or round denote(s) the number of stitches or spaces you should have on that row or round.

CROCHET TERMINOLOGY

UNITED STATES		INTERNATIONAL
slip stitch (slip st)	=	single crochet (sc)
single crochet (sc)	=	double crochet (dc)
half double crochet (hdc)	=	half treble crochet (htr)
double crochet (dc)	=	treble crochet (tr)
treble crochet (tr)	=	double treble crochet (dtr)
double treble crochet (dtr)	=	triple treble crochet (ttr)
triple treble crochet (tr tr)	=	quadruple treble crochet (qtr)
skip	=	miss

	LACE (0)	SUPER FINE (1)	FINE (2)	LIGHT (3)	MEDIUM (4)	BULKY (5)	SUPER BULKY (6)
Yarn Weight Symbol & Names							
Type of Yarns in Category	Fingering, 10-count crochet thread	Sock, Fingering Baby	Sport, Baby	DK, Light Worsted	Worsted, Afghan, Aran	Chunky, Craft, Rug	Bulky, Roving
Crochet Gauge* Ranges in Single Crochet to 4" (10 cm)	32-42 double crochets**	21-32 sts	16-20 sts	12-17 sts	11-14 sts	8-11 sts	5-9 sts
Advised Hook Size Range	Steel*** 6,7,8 Regular hook B-1	B-1 to E-4	E-4 to 7	7 to I-9	I-9 to K-10.5	K-10.5 to M-13	M-13 and larger

*GUIDELINES ONLY: The chart above reflects the most commonly used gauges and hook sizes for specific yarn categories.

** Lace weight yarns are usually crocheted on larger-size hooks to create lacy openwork patterns. Accordingly, a gauge range is difficult to determine. Always follow the gauge stated in your pattern.

*** Steel crochet hooks are sized differently from regular hooks–the higher the number the smaller the hook, which is the reverse of regular hook sizing.

CROCHET HOOKS

U.S.	B-1	C-2	D-3	E-4	F-5	G-6	H-8	I-9	J-10	K-10½	L-11	M/N-13	N/P-15	P/Q	Q	S
Metric - mm	2.25	2.75	3.25	3.5	3.75	4	5	5.5	6	6.5	8	9	10	15	16	19

◖▢▢▢ BEGINNER	Projects for first-time crocheters using basic stitches. Minimal shaping.
◖▮▢▢ EASY	Projects using yarn with basic stitches, repetitive stitch patterns, simple color changes, and simple shaping and finishing.
◖▮▮▢ INTERMEDIATE	Projects using a variety of techniques, such as basic lace patterns or color patterns, mid-level shaping and finishing.
◖▮▮◗ EXPERIENCED	Projects with intricate stitch patterns, techniques and dimension, such as non-repeating patterns, multi-color techniques, fine threads, small hooks, detailed shaping and refined finishing.

GAUGE

Exact gauge is essential for proper size. Before beginning your project, make the sample swatch given in the individual instructions in the yarn and hook specified. After completing the swatch, measure it, counting your stitches and rows/ rounds carefully. If your swatch is larger or smaller than specified, **make another, changing hook size to get the correct gauge**. Keep trying until you find the size hook that will give you the specified gauge.

JOINING WITH SC

When instructed to join with sc, begin with a slip knot on hook. Insert hook in stitch or space indicated, YO and pull up a loop, YO and draw through both loops on hook.

BACK LOOP ONLY

Work only in loop(s) indicated by arrow *(Fig. 2)*.

Fig. 2

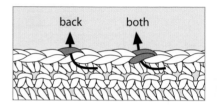

BACK RIDGE OF A CHAIN

Work only in the loops indicated by arrows *(Fig. 3)*.

Fig. 3

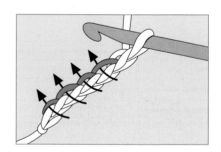

FREE LOOPS OF A CHAIN

When instructed to work in free loops of a chain, work in loop indicated by arrow *(Fig. 4)*.

Fig. 4

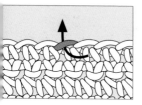

CHANGING COLORS

Insert hook in stitch indicated, YO and pull up a loop, cut yarn; with new yarn *(Fig. 5)*, YO and draw through both loops on hook.

Fig. 5

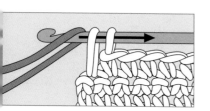

POST STITCH

Work around post of stitch indicated, inserting hook in direction of arrow *(Fig. 6)*.

Fig. 6

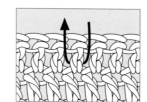

YARN INFORMATION

Each Blanket in this book was made using Light or Medium Weight Yarn. Any brand of Light or Medium Weight Yarn may be used. It is best to refer to the yardage/meters when determining how many balls or skeins to purchase. Remember, to arrive at the finished size, it is the GAUGE/TENSION that is important, not the brand of yarn. For your convenience, listed below are the specific yarns used to create our photography models.

ALTERNATING BLOCKS
Bernat® Softee® Baby
#02003 Lemon

RECTANGULAR FILET
Bernat® Softee® Baby
#02002 Pale Blue

CROSSED DOUBLES
Bernat® Softee® Baby
#02004 Mint

LEAF STITCH
Bernat® Softee® Baby
#30008 Antique White

RIPPLE
Bernat® Softee® Baby
White - #02000 White
Blue - #02002 Pale Blue

ZIG ZAG FILET
Bernat® Softee® Baby
#02001 Pink

MOUNTAINS & VALLEYS
Bernat® Softee® Baby
Pink - #02001 Pink
Blue - #02002 Pale Blue
White - #02000 White
Green - #02004 Mint
Yellow - #02003 Lemon

VERTICAL STRIPES
Bernat® Softee® Baby
Yellow - #02003 Lemon
White - #02000 White
Green - #02004 Mint

Production Team: Technical Writer/Editor - Linda A. Daley; Editorial Writer - Susan Frantz Wiles; Senior Graphic Artist - Lora Puls; Graphic Artist - Becca Snider Tally; Photo Stylists - Christy Myers and Lori Wenger; and Photographers - Mark Mathews and Ken West.